MUSICIANS
and THEIR
INSPIRATIONS

MILEY CYRUS and DOLLY PARTON

Two Tennessee Titans

Tom Jackson

Lerner Publications ◆ Minneapolis

Lerner Publications Company
An imprint of Lerner Publishing Group, Inc.
241 First Avenue North
Minneapolis, MN 55401 USA

For reading levels and more information, look up this title at www.lernerbooks.com.

Main body text set in Eurostile LT Pro.
Typeface provided by Linotype.

Library of Congress Cataloging-in-Publication Data

Names: Jackson, Tom, 1972- author.
Title: Miley Cyrus and Dolly Parton : two Tennessee titans / Tom Jackson.
Description: Minneapolis : Lerner Publications, 2024. | Series: Musicians and their inspirations | Includes bibliographical references and index. | Audience: Ages 8-12 | Audience: Grades 4-6 | Summary: "Miley Cyrus looks up to Dolly Parton. But Parton isn't just Cyrus's godmother-she's also her inspiration. From performing onscreen to creating music together, young readers learn more about their music, lives, and more"-- Provided by publisher.
Identifiers: LCCN 2023048478 (print) | LCCN 2023048479 (ebook) | ISBN 9798765626719 (library binding) | ISBN 9798765629123 (paperback) | ISBN 9798765635803 (epub)
Subjects: LCSH: Cyrus, Miley, 1992---Juvenile literature. | Parton, Dolly—Juvenile literature. | Singers—United States—Biography—Juvenile literature. | Country musicians—United States—Biography—Juvenile literature.
Classification: LCC ML3930.C98 J33 2024 (print) | LCC ML3930.C98 (ebook) | DDC 782.42164092/2 [B]—dc23/eng/20231013

LC record available at https://lccn.loc.gov/2023048478
LC ebook record available at https://lccn.loc.gov/2023048479

Manufactured in the United States of America

1 - CG - 7/15/24

TABLE OF CONTENTS

Introduction

Parton on the red carpet at the 2019 Grammys

In 2019, Dolly Parton received the MusiCares Person of the Year award at the Grammys. This award is given to artists for their achievements in music and charity work. Singers such as Katy Perry, Little Big Town, and more honored Parton on stage by singing her songs. However, the highlight of the night was when Parton took to the stage with Miley Cyrus. They sang "Jolene," one of Parton's biggest hits.

Cyrus's family is close friends with Parton. Cyrus is Parton's goddaughter. The young artist has known Parton her whole life. "Miley and I go back before she was even born," Parton said. "She's one of my favorite people."

The pair are no strangers to performing together, but the Grammy stage was one of their biggest shows yet. "There's a theory that you shouldn't meet your heroes," Cyrus said, "but I wish everyone had the chance to meet Dolly Parton because she's even better than your sparkliest dreams."

Cyrus singing "Jolene" with Parton at the 2019 Grammys

CHapTeR 1

Country Beginnings

Parton and Cyrus were both born and raised in Tennessee. Although they had very different childhoods, both became performers at a young age.

Parton was born in 1946 in Locust Ridge, Tennessee. Her father was a farmer. She had eleven brothers and sisters. The family didn't have much money growing up. Her mother often sang traditional folk songs from Great Britain to entertain the family. As a result, Parton discovered a love for music at a young age.

Parton started singing during church services when she was six. She was so good that she was invited to appear on local radio and television shows. When she was thirteen, Parton recorded her first single, "Puppy Love."

Parton became a professional singer after graduating from high school.

Greetings
FROM
NASHVILLE
★ TENNESSEE ★

Parton with Porter Wagoner during a recording of his television show in 1969

Moving to Nashville

After graduating high school, Parton wanted to work as a songwriter. She moved to Nashville, Tennessee, to find a career in music. She sang with and learned from an established country music singer, Porter Wagoner. In the 1970s, Parton became a solo artist and found lots of success. She quickly became one of the most popular country music singers in the US.

A Musical Childhood

Cyrus was born in 1992 in Nashville. She is the daughter of country-rock singer Billy Ray Cyrus. Through her dad, she often met famous musicians as a child, including Parton.

Cyrus at the Disney ABC TV All-Star Party in 2006

COOL CONNECTIONS

Billy Ray asked Parton to be his daughter's godmother. Parton prefers to think of herself as Cyrus's fairy godmother.

Cyrus and Billy Ray at the premiere of Hannah Montana: The Movie in 2009

Cyrus (center) and the other cast members of Hannah Montana in 2008

In 2006, Cyrus played the lead role on the Disney show *Hannah Montana*. She played Miley Stewart, an ordinary teenage kid, who has a secret life as a pop singer.

Cyrus recorded music and gave world tours for the show. After the show ended in 2009, Cyrus carried on with her musical career. Leaving the *Hannah Montana* character behind, Cyrus was free to try out all kinds of musical genres, such as rock, disco, and Parton's favorite, country.

Cyrus performing in New York City at Times Square

COOL CONNECTIONS

Parton (*left*) appeared alongside Cyrus (*center*) in *Hannah Montana* as a character called Aunt Dolly.

CHAPTER 2

Songs about Life

Cyrus and Parton both write their own songs based on their experiences in life. Parton's songs are mostly country. Cyrus's work includes many genres of music.

Parton has always been fascinated with rhythm and rhyme. Since she was young, she could latch onto a word or rhythm and write a song to go with it. She often draws on personal experience to write her lyrics.

When she was about eight, Parton started to write more serious songs. One of her first songs was inspired by a conversation she heard between her mom and aunts. It was about young men who had died during war. Parton often gets ideas for songs from stories. Some stories are her own, and some are those she observes in others. She then re-tells them in song.

Parton can play the guitar, violin, piano, and many other instruments.

THE LOVE ALBUM

I WILL ALWAYS LOVE YOU

YOU ARE

HEARTBREAKER

ONE OF THOSE DAYS

SEND ME THE PILLOW YOU DREAM ON

IT'S ALL WRONG, BUT IT'S ALL RIGHT

ISLANDS IN THE STREAM
(DUET WITH KENNY ROGERS)

JOLENE

THE BARGAIN STORE

HERE YOU COME AGAIN

LOVE IS LIKE A BUTTERFLY

COAT OF MANY COLOURS

PARTON

Hit Songs

Parton has said that she has written more than three thousand songs. Twenty-six were number-one singles in the country music chart. This includes "Coat of Many Colors," which was written about how her mother had once stitched rags together to make Parton a warm coat. Some of Parton's songs are famous for being performed by other musicians. One of Whitney Houston's most famous hits, "I Will Always Love You," was written by Parton.

GRAND OLE OPRY

TICKETS   THE OPRY SHOP

Tickets on sale for Parton's concert in Nashville

Parton performing in 2016 at Pittsburgh, Pennsylvania

INSPIRING THE INSPIRATION

AUNT DOROTHY JO

Parton grew up in a musical family. Her mother taught her the words and tunes for many songs. But Parton's biggest hero was her aunt Dorothy Jo. Dorothy Jo wrote songs to sing in church and played the banjo and guitar. "I saw myself in her, and do to this day," Parton said. "In my young teenage years, we started writing songs together."

Personal Stories

Cyrus compares her songwriting process to writing a diary entry. She writes about how she's feeling at that moment. Then she will add the melody and verses later. Like Parton, Cyrus's music is personal. She shares her stories through her songs. Then people experience her stories with her. "When people hear my music, they hear a fragment of time, something I feel or felt right then," she says.

COOL CONNECTIONS

Parton's 2023 album, *Rockstar,* is her first move into rock music. The album includes Cyrus's hit song "Wrecking Ball," which the pair sing together.

Cyrus goes on world tours to sing for her fans around the globe.

CHAPTER 3

Making an Appearance

With her iconic fashion choices, Parton is one of the most recognizable singers in the world. At the same time, Cyrus is constantly evolving her style.

As a singer in 1960s Nashville, Parton wore colorful stage clothes inspired by dresses worn by people in mountain communities. Later, she wanted to appeal to a wider audience. She introduced more glamor to her outfits. She often wears gold or silver outfits covered in sequins. It is common for her clothes to have tassel fringes. Parton is also well-known for her iconic blonde hair.

On stage, the focus is on Parton's voice. She has a band and backup singers. She sometimes plays piano or guitar too. Often, she'll walk around the stage to engage the audience. Parton will also invite singers on stage to perform duets.

Parton wears bright clothes that stand out on stage.

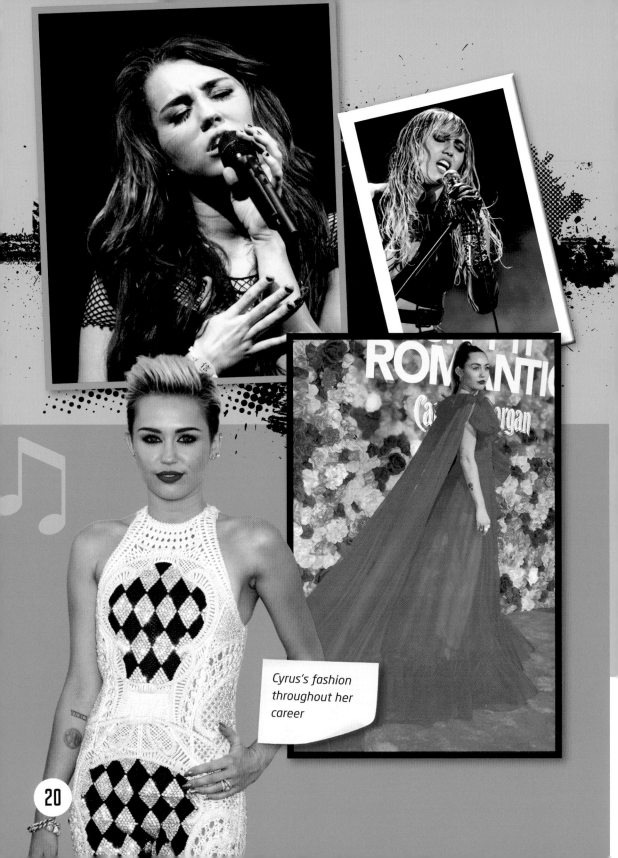

Cyrus's fashion throughout her career

Style Icon

Cyrus's fashion styles and performances have changed many times over her career. She started out as a teen pop star who wore simple, everyday clothes like her young fans. With her fourth album, *Bangerz*, Cyrus went for an older look, cutting her hair short and wearing revealing outfits.

Cyrus sings "Someone Else" on a stage prop during the Bangerz tour in 2014.

Cyrus performing on TV in 2017

In 2017, Cyrus returned to her musical roots with country, pop, and rock in her album *Younger Now*. Parton sang with Cyrus on the song "Rainbowland." In Cyrus's live performances, she wore simple denim stage clothes and cowgirl hats.

COOL CONNECTIONS

Parton and Cyrus have both acted in films. Parton played a role in the 1980 film *9 to 5*. Cyrus starred in the film *The Last Song* from 2010.

New Looks

Then in 2020, Cyrus's style changed again with her album *Plastic Hearts*. Cyrus chose a synth pop and rock sound influenced by the 1980s. The album cover also drew inspiration from punk fashion from this time. In 2023, Cyrus released a dance album, *Endless Summer Vacation*, in yet another shift of direction in the way the artist presented herself. The album features upbeat tracks with lyrics reflecting on her life and relationships.

Cyrus wearing an outfit created by Gucci in 2021

23

CHAPTER 4

Country Royalty

After so many years in the spotlight, Parton is one of the most successful musicians of all time. Cyrus has been working for fewer years but has made a large impact in the industry.

Parton's success is in large part due to the effort she's put in. She has sold more than 100 million records over her career. Many of her songs chart on the Billboard 100.

Since her career took off, she has been nominated for a Grammy fifty-one times, winning eleven of them. Parton is also one of only six women to win the Academy of Country Music's Entertainer of the Year award. Two of Parton's songs were nominated for an Oscar. In 2001, she was inducted into the Songwriter's Hall of Fame.

Parton at the Academy of Country Music Awards in 2016

COOL CONNECTIONS

Both singers work for charity. Cyrus set up the Happy Hippie Foundation to support LGBTQ+ members, young people without homes, and people who are vulnerable in other ways. Parton works with the Dollywood Foundation to help Tennessee children get a good education.

Global Star

Cyrus's albums often chart on the Billboard 100. Although one of her biggest hits was the 2013 song "Wrecking Ball," Cyrus has not stopped there. She constantly changes up her music and style for fans. Cyrus has also gone on five world tours, performing to more than half a million fans. Cyrus has won several MTV awards and has been honored with many other awards for her work as an actor and musician.

Cyrus draws influence from many people around her, including her biggest inspiration, Parton. But she's also not afraid to take her music in new directions. With a future of endless possibilities in front of her, Cyrus is taking the reins in her life.

Cyrus at the 2023 Versace fashion show in Los Angeles, California

Your Inspiration

Parton became a chart-topping songwriter and powerful female force in country music during a time when the industry was run mostly by men. She later became a source of support for Cyrus in her musical and acting career.

Cyrus has been through a lot of changes in her career as she transformed from a teen pop star to world-class musician. Sometimes people complained about her new musical styles and fashion choices. However, like Parton before her, Cyrus is not afraid to try out new things.

Who inspires you? They don't have to be someone famous. It could be anyone: your best friend, your teacher, your aunt, or a person in your community. Why do they inspire you? What can you learn from them?

IMPORTANT DATES

1959   Dolly Parton records her first single, "Puppy Love."

1980   Parton stars in the film *9 to 5*.

2001   Parton is inducted into the Songwriter's Hall of Fame.

2006–9   Miley Cyrus stars in the Disney television show *Hannah Montana*.

2013   Cyrus releases "Wrecking Ball," her biggest hit so far.

2017   Cyrus releases the album *Younger Now*, in which Parton sings on the song "Rainbowland."

2019   Parton and Cyrus perform together at the Grammy Awards.

2023   Parton releases her forty-ninth studio album, *Rockstar*. Cyrus releases a dance album, *Endless Summer Vacation*.

GLOSSARY

country: a form of popular music that comes from the Southern and Southwestern United States

duet: a song sung by two singers

evolve: to undergo change

genre: a style of music

glamor: something that is exciting, especially in fashion

godmother: a person who is asked by a child's parents to look after and offer mentorship to the child

iconic: widely recognizable

LGBTQ+: short for lesbian, gay, bisexual, transgender, queer, and other sexual, romantic, or gender identities

nominate: to name or be included in a competition to win an award

solo: a song that is sung by one person

synth: short for *synthesizer* and refers to an electronic musical instrument

SOURCE NOTES

5   Waleed Aly, "Dolly Parton Reveals How Close To Miley Cyrus She Really Is," *The Project*, July 6, 2023, https://www.youtube.com/watch?v=YJaC-tglj6k.

5   Miley Cyrus, "Dolly Parton," *Time*, September 15, 2021, https://time.com/collection/100-most-influential -people-2021/6096090/dolly-parton.

15   Kelsey Goeres, "Dolly Parton's Biggest Influences Weren't Big 'Stars'," Showbiz CheatSheet, April 6, 2021, https://www.cheatsheet.com/entertainment/dolly -parton-biggest-influences-werent-big-stars.html.

16   Miley Cyrus, "Miley Cyrus's Personal Memo to the World," *Vanity Fair*, February 21, 2019, https://www.vanityfair.com /style/2019/02/miley-cyrus-personal-memo-to-the-world.

LEARN MORE

Britannica Kids: Dolly Parton
https://kids.britannica.com/students/article/Dolly-Parton/312908

Britannica Kids: Miley Cyrus
https://kids.britannica.com/students/article/Miley-Cyrus/470864

Dolly Parton: Official Website
https://dollyparton.com/

Hannah Montana: Official Website
https://shows.disney.com/hannah-montana

Holleran, Leslie. *Dolly Parton: Diamond in a Rhinestone World.* Minneapolis: Lerner Publications, 2023.

Moening, Kate. *Dolly Parton: Country Music Star.* Minneapolis: Bellwether Media, 2021.

Rose, Rachel. *Dolly Parton: Singer and Cultural Icon.* Minneapolis: Bearport Publishing, 2023.

INDEX

PHOTO ACKNOWLEDGMENTS

Image credits: Kathy Hutchins/Shutterstock.com, pp. 4, 19c, 20c, 20d, 25; Rob Latour/Shutterstock, p. 5; © 1977 RCA Records/Wikimedia Commons, p. 7a; Callahan/Shutterstock.com, p. 7b; © 968 Moeller Talent, Inc. Nashville/Wikimedia Commons, p. 8; Featureflash Photo Agency/Shutterstock.com, p. 9a; s_bukley/Shutterstock.com, pp. 9b, 10a; Joe Seer/Shutterstock.com, p. 10b; Everett Collection/Shutterstock.com, p. 11a; Disney Channel/Kobal/Shutterstock, p. 11b; Dennis Carney/Wikimedia Commons, p. 13a; defotoberg/Shutterstock.com, p. 13b; Paul Mckinnon/Dreamstime.com, p. 14a; Jack Fordyce/Shutterstock.com, p. 14b; Skyhawk/Shutterstock.com, p. 15a; Gyvafoto/Shutterstock.com, p. 15b; Vereshchagin Dmitry/Shutterstock.com, p. 15c; calmdownlove/Flickr.com/Wikimedia Commons, p. 17a; Gilles Mingasson/ABC/Shutterstock, p. 17b; Debby Wong/Shutterstock.com, p. 17c; Wirestock Creators/Shutterstock.com, p. 19a; Featureflash Photo Agency/Shutterstock.com, p. 19b; Sam Borowski/Flickr.com/Wikimedia Commons, p. 20a; Brian Friedman/Shutterstock.com, p. 20b; Rob Sinclair/Flickr.com/Wikimedia Commons, p. 21; Mass Communication Specialist 3rd Class Casey J. Hopkins/Flickr.com/Wikimedia Commons, p. 22; Tinseltown/Shutterstock.com, p. 23; Matt Baron/BEI/Shutterstock, p. 26. Cover: Gustavo Miguel Fernandes/Shutterstock.com; Adam Shanker/Shutterstock.com.